Hungry Slingshots

Hungry Slingshots

Louis Cabri

Vancouver | New Star Books | 2020

NEW STAR BOOKS LTD.
www.NewStarBooks.com | info@NewStarBooks.com
107-3477 Commercial St., Vancouver, BC V5N 4E8 CANADA
1574 Gulf Rd., No. 1517, Point Roberts, WA 98281 USA

The publisher acknowledges the financial support of the Government of Canada throught the Canada Book Fund and the Canada Council for the Arts and the British Columbia Arts Council.

Cataloguing information for this book is available from Library and Archives Canada, www.collectioncanada.gc.ca

Cover design by Oliver McPartlin.
Printed and bound in Canada by Imprimerie Gauvin, Gatineau, QC.
First printing April 2020

CONTENTS

This book is for Nicole

Vireo Goes Whip Tim Kelly

justlearning: Who's Tim Kelly?

one; two; three; four; six
hip; hip; hip hurrah boys; spring is here
chortle-deeeeee

chew-chew-chew
listen to my evening sing-ing-ing-ing
tic-tic-mcgreer

shook-shook-shook-shook-shook
je-je-je-je-je-je-je
pill-will-willet

ra-vi-o-li
kit
cheer-up; cheer-a-lee; cheer-ee-o

whoo-eek
jeeeeeeee
check

click click (typewriter-like)
oh; dear me! (three blind mice)
where are you? and here I am

too-too-too
who's awake? me too
here-here; where-where; all-together-down-the-hill

who-cooks-for-you; who-cooks-for-you-all
(a ping-pong ball dropped onto a table increasing in rate and pitch)
pleased-pleased-pleased-pleased-ta-meetcha

but-I-DO-love-you
I'm-I'm-I'm-so-sweet
sweet; sweet; sweet; little-more-sweet

quick give me a rain check
qu'est-ce qu'il dit? qu'est-ce qu'il dit?
cover-it-up; pull-it-up; pull-it-up

come here Jimmy quickly
spit and see if I care; spit
Madge; Madge; Madge pick beetles off; the water's hot

here; here; come right here; dear
quick; three-beers
fire; fire; where? where? here; here; see it? see it?

hurry; worry; blurry; flurry
more; more; more cheezies; please pink
drop-it; drop-it; cover-it-up

dear; dear; dear
here; here; here peter-peter-peter
po-ta-to-chip (and dip)

kicky-chew; kiki-krrr; pee-pee-toe
see-bit-see-bit-see-bit
see-see-see-see

gulp; gulp; gulp
hot dog; pickle-ickle-ickle
chuck chuck chuck-it-too-ee zhew zhew

I am so laz-eeeeee
please; please; please squeeeeze
t-cheer; t-cheer; t-cheer

cheer-cheer-cheer-purty-purty-purty
chip-chewy-chew
veer-veer-veer-veer

skaip
chatter
eh-eh; eh-eh

ah; ah; ah; ah
few
pee-trip-treee

tu-tu-tu
spring-of-the-year
no hope

haa-haa-haa-haa
wuff; wuff; wuff; wuff; wuff
tree; tree; tree terwitter-witter wit

tea-kettle; tea-kettle; tea-kettle
pit-sit
tee-seep

turdle; turdle; turdle; two-to-you
twit-twit-twit; sweet-sweet-sweet
zweet; zweet; zweet

yoo-yoo; yoo-yoo-yoo
shaaaaack paark
Pe-cos; Pe-cos; Pe-cos

THE MOMMY COLLECTION

After *Roses de Noël* (1843-1878) by Théodore de Banville

It seemed the only thing you could do is crawl under
the bed, and start saying, over and over
and over again: I want my mommy. Mommy
mommy. Please, make it stop, mommy, I don't
like this. Mommy, this is very bad.
—Errol Morris

TEAR SQUISHER

If you don't see the face of your son
Under the crate (delivered by a professional)
If for you the child you sawed and hammered to sleep
Remains a crate, then Mum

Let me get stoned on the smoking resin, your voice, again
My poetic, my first sleepover
Kneeling here beside you
Rest my head on the skirt flap

I want to become a blubberer again, I do
Forgetting the touch-screen, be RE-LIVED
When a comb'd gently pass through my hair
A golden one — from fairyland!

At your hand folding down my lids
I'd waken, stoned
Euphoric, tingling, nourished
In the empty, dry volume

Cadencing motes
Darkdreaming alongside you
I want to reflect on pouts again and that when I get high
I'm a bitter somnambulist

You used to say: My son, one day you'll suffer
Let's put off the bad
Hide in my arms
And those kisses I received

This category of France's "lie"
We both knew
Made their truth
Yes, the only! And now, I hallucinate

Mum! — let me say that word
Charm and let forget — there is nothing except this moment
If I'm happy again
When I forget and when I cry

YOUR ATTENTIONAL ANNUITY

Murmurings among the living
Room dribblers
Distracting your attention from *me*
While the fire's in there happy shining up the chimney's ass
A fugitive discreetly appears
At window, chuckling, wheezing — a John Candy —
Spring

Impatient and bearing enormous gifts
I promise you . . . a *renaissance*
Look at Spring! Unable to modernize
You'd think from the hopping around, has *really* got to pee
Twitching in the rain, lifting bits of its foliage, entreats
With — droopy lightbeams

Mum, consoler of anyone, yes because of you
Nature reddening despairs in truth and law
Who's complicit? Yours truly
Therefore resolves to be Nature no more
Offer instead my seasonal first
Murmurings among the living
Room dribblers

Lillydale — No Taint!

What with whining and snot ropes ahoy, bending
Over vomit and steadying bitter saltwaves
Craning for eyes — dear Mum's!
Our all-englobing sphere — sparkles in our mist
"Axis: bold as love" — we suffer it: cornerstore roasting spit

Out of storm and wind, an exemplary icon glistens
Lillydale ham parts the skies, an offer
Booms above, "Slice?"
Grip firmly, keep heady, mother (such sovereignty . . .)
Serene pinkness, no taint!

Ros and Carlet

A few wintry flowers ... that's it, Mum. Petals
Do you remember the petal? Won't open, that buttony thing
Gorgeous to you, better than words
Conjure gardens

Before the eyes, they didn't turn
Camry to corolla
Burning ROS and carlet
Two pieces of water, one telephone pole, *verdure*

See it
Hair / floating / veils / laughter — is that
A metaplasm Frenchist
The way Spring watercolours?

I love the signal-strength: no static overmuch, nor too-little felt
    at a distance. My mother!
That look, softer than museum poster Impressionism
Makes treacle out of Theo's poems — sovereign remedy
Sky shows its dawn crack, smiling, up yours, Society

Nature's Calvinist calling, if one day traipsing in haughty canyons
    I'm out of drinking water
I'll owe you — that's you, Mum
High on a pulsing fountain chant
In TD square, I know, you're Nature's extreme sport

The ductile words we savoured disordered
Them drawn is what counted for charm, "Old wheel potter, whew!"
You gave me your very own evasions — in looks — my own
    modeling clay — books —
Hug again your son who cries at your knees

CORRUPTING WET

To kiss prairie stubble and the drowning river
          Rolling its own reflections
Glides a queer lightbeam, furtive
          Among blackening branches, trailing

Flowers want to charge for the light — dear to us
          In green foam
Under gentle breezes
          Pink petals wink open, winter ellipsis

Oh that mourning find its piece —
          For revenge — !
Decrepit children
          Stalk again, thang rhythm, Americacetera

O adored look our looks plunge in
          So long as she's the look — if'n't, then
We did not live, we did not cry
          The rest, Canadacetera

So long as we pressed you in our arms by turns
          Battered up
Our remote inner poodles, we forgot the rest, bounding love
          Wired on corrupting wet, shocks etcetera

Song-Chamber

La Breeze, harsh-rose charmer, that single zephyr
Frigged the blond sea into flame and sapphire
(Thus the ocean's song-chamber off the Florida Keys)

Oh, tell me, you both must know, how do you keep fat
Loveliness, grace, and vivacity, Spring
(Ocean's resounding chamber — just off the Keys) Hmmm?

When I'm brushed into the corner by brooming
Youth lands a lunar module on the soft features of your face
(Ocean's song-chamber resounding off the Florida Keys)

Azure thinks with seas and skies of the boldest airs
Also your eyes, Mum, they think: *Azure*
(This ocean's song-chamber — Ken Nordine on the Keys)

Ennobling loves the dittany of health
And youth can land a lunar module in winter sun, rarefied light
(Thus the ocean's song-chamber off the Florida Keys)

The Mother Contends With the Sky

Skies alive — forty
Billion tons young, from the deep end of enchanted carbonic
    shadow
Sootpuff on cheek: a charmer, friend-of-family, La Breeze

Dust up, birds wriggle
And we flip
Pictures, and cry

Stars
Reflected with lacrimal reflex
by lysozymic propulsion due to an errant wingtip?

A distant spectral emulsion
Salves the anticipation and solitude
Of tears

Nursing 101

You know it: adoration of the mother
Because we got souls because she looked, because she looked out
        for us
No sweetener! "The client may feel you're not interested"

All the way to you, mom, left to your driving
Our wishes fly from the superchannels
Of sweeteners — "The client may feel you're not interested"

That post-post-New Left Love divides again aesthetics from
        ideology critique
Ablaze woke
Unsweetening (hold the exclamation mark) ("The client may feel
    you're not interested" (release the exclamation mark))

Reparable roadways! All the same, no sidewalk, no trees
Sky pulls blankets of particulate up to cirrus — goodnight
To trusting a human face — with your force, your joy

Nursing 101 — "The client may feel you're not interested"
That they look out for you, mum
Sweetener or no

AFRICAN VIOLETS

Animating one more conversation — potted
African violets . . . I'm begging you . . . on my knees —
Let that Timbits oded Instagrammer
With the attack-narcissism of "bite-sized blasts of flavour"
Try sweetening your frail cot breath
Or — that gassy Beatquik, Celliniesque braggadocio of silver
Screen descriptions, *There's a path to a river view*
Between these fenced estates, These lilies are for you —
Let him do the sending love, in verse
Try intelligible form
"Loquent, lettered, punctuated"
"A most tender denotation"
What, don't you know this guy?
Mum, it's me
Mum, when snow finally locks the door
You imagine me, ok?
Suturing strophes into snow
Flakes and crying winds
Haphazard pursuits, chimerical
Wonder — my mother

Useless!

I think, therefore because of you —
Disturbed — it's you — the dream, white-robed behind bars
What could I do then
How

O charmed, attentive guardian — now under guard
Source of all streaming — now lost
And that it's my turn and nothing's turned
Nothing — not even nothing

Heart
Useless
Tendernesses these, loves these
Useless!

As Bees Vaulting the Forehead of a Cow

The mother who assuages lack of nerve
And idling
Stands outside that splintery place she rests in at night
Props branching hydrangea
Collects licheny twigs from neighbouring trees
Restive leaves cry to be held also in the lively flurry
Roaming attentions and happiness animating strangers
O face
          Between us shut
Doors, much noise, many cities'
Time machines — which times? *times*, and *nights*
Which? just say to her *nights* — days? say *days*
And about silence? what silence, only *silence* — and of space, *space*
And for hills, *hills* For *Woods*, for *Skies*, for *Winds* . . .
Your outside, mother, when even inside, caring for an ant.
Soon enough, a small bird's compass
Will be the eyes that sparkle for it — like yours.
Birds will have quickened to me
(I'm far from home, too)
Singing: From out of the blue, this obscurity, "poet"
One day'll disappear like us
Let's lend the outsourced mechanic song
For the year to come, he may delight
As bees vaulting the forehead of a cow —
Soon, mother
Birds and beasts
Joyful
At your window

Unsentimental in the Legal Sense

Tweetie Bird nestings
Flowers and branches

Abhors kitty photos
Unsentimental in the legal sense

Murder in the first degree
He who is absent comical

"From a dark and angry place"
A letter to the editor: Re! Post-Office! Delivery!

Whipping up seas without horizon
Children inconsolably glum, drowned

Brats' rules birthdays' roles
The mum treatment for Mum

Opens a window, Spring's witness, at least
To kiss cheeks

Ruffle hills' green beard
Soon — tomorrow even — melting ice

La Breeze floats
Careens, I don't know whose invisible caress

Touch of damp blanket
From shivering skies, bird and beast joy

Charms the blues blue, speaks of clemency
Utopia perfume

Mother
    Coddles to sleep with
A triumphant
    Refrain

"Make
    Liberals
Cry
    Again"

From
    Childhood —
"Triumphant
    Childhood"

And
    Like her, it's
A 24-hr
    Surveil when

A crowd
    Walks
Into
    Blood sport

For those
    Who
Charm the
    Sleepwalk

"Make
    Liberals
Cry
    Again"

The adult
   Still child
They praise as
   She did, Mum

THE BROMELIAD

*Some individuals spend their whole lives in
and around bromeliad pools.*

One more sensitive

plant, soil

poured
with chemicals — and there

goes

"there goes"

again . . . more compact
form

than the passive "poured" —

the agent did knock,

a meeting did happen,
some performatives

did (felicity conditions — met)
sign off:

     all, contractual detail, except

and heregoes the next
caveat, just swimming in them

the way language use isn't linear
history, but the way the history

encrusting language users
rotted off them, the information Google, the ruling Grace,
        collects, flake by flake,

data exhaust from the speech organ
till the thick stalk stuck —

while its measurements are toured
for a factory with the right fit —

like a stake,

and out of the cups of the heavy flowers

emptied the rain of the thunder-showers.

Once more, sensitive plant.

Does Odes

Someone, I guess, broke
the green flag-like tips

on the gone brown plant?
Palm reader,

your physics, please.
What was

not alive, now is
dying.

O tenebrous murk, neon
shingle. Cryptic

parade. Branching out
from

human palm. To plant.
Potted likes:

low, indirect light.
The juice temporarily paralyses

the vocal chords.
Can you talk?

It called.
That's right, it's impersonal.

Impersonal pronoun. Distinguishes from
the imperial single

measure
I.

It called.
Interior life. January 29th.

Any here
hear of one?

History catch-up might
includes: Invented

street
lighting

eventually
toaster.

Antenna and
interior — inter-

changeable
reception

as
in does

that sound — *that*
sound attune

enough? It's an adz.
Chop.

Any here
seen one?

Geographic
might in clues.

My how your y
loops and g

loops round. "I'm
such a

wolf," says
little red.

Chop.
Whatever's eating whose

world, "Help it grow" . . . ?
Chop.

Read this then (2:01 pm)
write that

then
then I change completely, after I move —

didn't tell you ("you"?) that part?
that and then I write

then that happens . . .
Then that happens . . . the call, the secret

policed, I'd
fear

wonder
itself — What *did* I

write.
Chop!

Gone!
That's what writing like

this way is — the hand
doodle in

pencil
wood to scrap

paper, babbling,
untitled

acts —
coming to.

Conscious
to *that* extent, some

letters, sure, and
their sounds

made
"as

in does" . . . adz
as in

ads as
in

adds good but
the *monitoring*

social
media platform

paranoia and *conspiracy*
take-aways —

what stresses. On this tressle?
Wanted to ask . . . do you

like toast? prefer
the lit

bulb — electric — to
burning lumps of grease? Do you think

we need *working*
hospitals

as in
does —

precisely:
the "as"

is *in*
"does," the doing

as
in *does*

science.
Therefore chop?

They somehow agreed, many times
in many languages —

windows, plants
indoors feel

— that all of it
called,

fabled sounds
crackling, fires,

and to
calling it,

I'm a chorus
of its,

in "the historical record"
one thing.

Chop.
Take

dose, skate.
The plants stake

town by
handshake

sculptured fibreglass
gold in city garden.

Now dying?
To quote: It's not impersonal.

Tasty … Tasty!

how come

hm …

— Hm!———

   say tornadoes, but you, swear, read
   "tornadoes," what

   a
   SHAM, I mean, SHAME

   that, shame it now, sham it
   updid you

   know you're
   quoting

   your hidden quoting shall
   am

   um
   om

   al-Sham
   shazam WAIT these

   words

      keep breaking
      up, two

      breaks
      down

one floating "shall
am" persists, whaaaat, it's like

NAME
your

place
INDICTED

   (*all* the law
   shows say it

   this way, in-DYTE, Laura
   Proudfoot

   blog comment
   Merriam-Webster's)

by
wind & going in wrong

directions for speech & company, backwards
on the horse in

a supplement, preposition to
company speech

elsewhere
sensation along neck, care raising

   tornado with lairs letters
   the "mean do" tercet "I

   mean do
   I"

question-mark tornado with layers later to mean with
        Letters to
"dim lands of peace": "stands

for
peas" your

quoting face, role of the tongue, roll-off
face

roll your faceroll away for
it WAIT these

bargainings words
keep

                until, finally, *finally*, there's
                listless

                set
                to

                lay about
                a

                table of elements
                "minimal, discrete"

                upon resistant micrologic
                (repels *and* breathes)

                because
                we're *not* faceless units (which we are)

                we're, say
                it's . . . Value

Village (can't
be

they say
led

or set
even

to
table — bad

manners
bad

cliché days
these

waiting words
keep these

words —

    Stroganoff
    means
    comes in a can (*stroke one off for Stro———!*)

    the way jihad doesn't
    mean
    striving

    or
    is "mum"
    "mom"

    does
    aloof rhyme
    with

a roof
mean
house

dog
what do
you call that a

knob
turned to get
water in

sink if there isn't one
cow hump — !———
how come

hm . . .
Hm!———
it's like

"whaaaat" — whaaaat———
like
is it?

how come

hm . . .

— Hm!———

Hail — to the Brails

July 28 2018, closer to
World War
Two with

every pronouncement, this one
asserted, soon
One. And then beyond

the kitsch &
absurd to some
earlier "ground"

high-definition
Zero?
Stacked

1/

against: a plaint
                of waffles.
Honeys upon the head after

noon sleep in sun

flame barber.
You know?

How can you dislike the word moist.

You're an astronaut
you know.

But the forecastle's

full, full of modern castles.

Pirate hails
from foredinghy.
Wind picks up frigate

bird by its pinions, legs
momentarily relax.

Too short to fall, I drown.

Peanut shells

in with yellow tulips

in sleet —

I caw.

You know.

Parse the service job please
to the non-serviceables
part mutations feel.

The fake is not fake, but the real
is not real (I could read this in anyone's poem

counter-pronouncement. What I mean

Well, I'm not going to get too in-the-weeds on this. Oh sure.
July forestry report. Current number
engulfed in salt water

has Bermuda cherry on top. There are back issues.
Know what I mean?
In the town of blank, dogs drink the rain.

In Camembert village a bib
the size of the town of blank molders in a laundry basket.
You know?

There's a crockery of snow piling in the city perimeter
as Souster Country writes the big dishwasher in the sky.
But as a mechanic — Freud's early model.

Impedimentary, my backup valve.
Know what I mean? Staid waiter nods here.
"Bundes." Excuse me. What?

2/

or against: Dirt bike clutch
matching trail incline degree by degree until
over backwards.

What should *I* do.
Expression bringing with it a flavour profile.
Ta-daaa! Art.

Generous with the lettuce, you.
It's a light lunch.
But jam's in the jar, jars on the shelf, shelves in the store visible

through closed door window, taped
paper on it saying
Wait Wait Don't Tell Me.

You know?
Chiming in? Use chimes.
Burp, burp, burp one million

six hundred thousand eighteen, three hundred
thirty views of *nothin.*
Oh they heard.

Clean and airy
venue out passenger jet porthole

skewed inside economy.
Bra cup for coffee filter.
Sweeter smoke

pepperiness traditional Maritime notes.
Marsdust on barnhog.
Balding -jectives

beyond the stall
phooey.
Do you know what I mean?

FLAGS OF CONVENIENCE

The argument

"Celebration," Kool & the Gang; Detroit River, Nov 2014, "Live Ships Map – Vessel Traffic and Positions," MarineTraffic.com; "Can Canada duplicate its boat people rescue with Syrian refugees?" Peter Goodspeed, TheStar.com, Fri Sep 26 2014; Darlene Keju, "Speech to World Council of Churches, Vancouver 1983," Youtube

Kaye E. Barker

OK, you are now chairwoman of the Marystown Chapter

Come on!

abandoned his book on 'Haykel' and founded Operation Lifeline

Ce-le-brex time

(Zo-loft!)

Federal Kumano

Zoloft Apartments

Asteline Reunion Hall

Asteline!

Oh Asteline

leeward Howard Adelman

Algosoo

Treximet
Prozatene idle

Nexium
Catullus

Catullus

Sarah Desgagnés

Levitrain chaintion Vioxx way

Federal Kumano

Nexium comparator
Pristiq

Pristiq bounty

Kimono Condoms

Lavoris orange (sponge)

Vytorin head plate

Rebecca Lynn plate

Retaphin dolphination

Orsula

via cargo

ship interview

ing people

fallout

Abilify
jest

club Abilify
jelly Vioxx sway

calendrical

Darlene Keju

Humira ship
ping container Zoloft apartments

Crestor, tanker

Focalin

Ken Boothe Sr

He's also moved to the absolute top of his class in all subjects
(excerpt for his writing lol)

Vyvanse

Vyvanse!

Federal Kumano

Cymbalta union

Niaspan incursive

Dick Beddoes

Kimono

Condo minimums

hull strength at full draught

Advair

Nair

pristine

ninnity

in *add*

year none

of us spoke

English pass

partout

Viet name ease, Syrian plea

Come on

BEFORE THE LEASE OF DEMOCRACY LISTED DEMOCRACY LISTED

with Rob Manery

ideomatic murmur:
"Walmart patrols!"

    contuse
    enantiodromes

reactive regionalisms
here

    regional nationalisms
    arbitrary

capitals
breach of puffery

    salute destitute
    or *really* merely

impoverished
solace

    of phones
    fawning optics

walrus sheds
an eye

    car parker eats it
    job hunting

snark
bleat

"covenant!"
nascent coercion

smartcard commons
surveilled

makes
of theory

hors d'oeuvres
from out of work —

it takes
a loan . . .

— to out of text
pleasure

monuments
of the opiate

moment
out accumulates

numinous non-moment
blindfolds breather

cross-eyed pained
lapses

never all
safe

jet ink particles part
more theories

of partition this
sunned hummer

merely a hurt
my, my

    hey, hey
    head-proof

— plugs work
sense

    sides with sliding scale
    steepens take

home
insult in

    an insistence:
    weal cut

depends on
a blue John Deere

    in stern
    steer clear-O

fabricate jeering under
privilege

    edged scant
    menu leave

canned want
for the podcast

    serial glare
    on every plate

a number
to licensed makes

        "strong sense" takes
        rhymed

swollen precision
package acronym

        inheritance trance
        before the burn of democracy blisters

democracy filibusters
slugger

        down the birth canal
        a union bleats

of a beanstalk
montage

        opens
        see-me feel-me

ceded
to sesame ringleader

        proposes sawed-off
        illocution

spiteful sermons
no eeeee!

        nor mobility —
        reneged — affront

resold bus transfer
(exchange variation)

        twizzler drops
        rain puddle

sad day
twiddler puzzles

      idle scruples
      re-dressed regret

sidled activism
shucked reconciliation

      greets aphoristic
      apology

an official
panto

      punted by the PMO
      patents who

can say
publicly

      they anticipate
      cement sounds mixing

misstep
warded nor

      thwarted
      neither

"nor"
logical

      here : extender
      car : bender

toe : barber
golf : Scots Doric

        standard
        poor index

plods past worn
parades

        glazed codex
        legitimate swindle

housed scorned
cipher, this

        Kodaked mammalian
        lament:

night of the living
syntax,

        murmurs of
        moon rocks.

Origins of a Style: World Summit

(It's not often that I give credit to the crowd)
"Suffice it to say"

     "Suffice it to say" — the verb tense here (one I am also
       fond of) cuts through the layers of history —
     What had you been thinking about

letting go of the Riot Within, by telling my story
So much style and it's wastin'

     I go on loving you like water
     As Jameson comments, it is as though a kind of
       repressed foundational longing found its way back
       into writing

the face studiously bloodied
Rain falls in drops, and there are many of them, and particularly
     noticeable — their direction: all languages speak of rain *falling*

     Rain is the crowd in the moment of discharge
     There's also some kind of diamond-shaped groove in
       the baton that leaves a horrible cut in the skin

Clymer made waves by sharing the story of how the cops had
     blatantly showed me off around the precinct in my beat-up
     state
. . . and stands also for the crowd's attenuation

     I seek (the vulgarization of theory itself) to use their
       rhetoric without suggesting some ultimate lack of
       referent or indeterminacy for writing
     You were not elected President

Unfortunately, the thought secreted in the brain cannot subsist
        when that which produces it no longer exists
On ne naît pas femme

            When you read it was sincere the coasts
            stammered

I favour the rhetoric of hyperbole here because exaggeration opens
        up a space for deliberation otherwise closed to the discreet or
        subtle reading
(It's hard to pick the crowd of the year, I wasn't *in* them? but, ·
        from afar . . .)

            "Thus"
                            the calls . . .

I worry
I had dropped out and bartended

            (People freakin' stayed up til 4 am, so I gotta give
                    props)
            "Henceforth"

why of course reflecting all
mystery you don't want surrounded the real

                anxiety here in this writing is also unprofessional
                (The great people of that great city came out)

"fun-park"
What fun-park?

            "Indeed,"
            (They had *no reason* to come out, but they came out
                    early)

We call for a general strike, around the country, and around the
    world
The name of the young activist they were interviewing in the
    streets of Oakland, California in November 2011 as Louise
    Michel

        "More properly"
                    or the porch chairs
will teach you about men
(They were packed to the rafters)

            But this is to proceed as though there were nothing
                problematic or obscure
            Any model of clear and inductive writing would
                suggest that now is not the point to regress
                further from whatever point I am supposed to be
                making here

Is there a class struggle in this text?
The critic Georges Lecomte noticed, writing in 1891, the static
    quality of the audience, that in Seurat's *Cirque* the spectators
    watching the show remain completely impassive, they have
    stereotyped faces and poses

            Happiness does not wait to leave, as poets note
            "Must"

(Loud, they showed love)
it is contagious and insatiable, it can break out anywhere, and with
    great suddenness, it is multiple, it is destructive, it has an
    enemy, it dies, it acts as though it were alive and is so treated

            reading it carelessly as if to tell you your fears were
                justified
            "All"

Everything, everywhere is flammable, and anything can be a spark
All this is true of the crowd

HOW to get into synthesiser position
"Sheer"

around that dubious adolescent class-position the "bookworm"
(And they gobbled up the tickets rather quickly)

    darkness in the hole
    "Cries out"

(One of the top three crowds ever, literally, probably)
"Hitherto"

    (This one, to me, was . . . Honestly, I had it down to
        two)
    "Clearly"

They could all go home now the hole was dark
(I thought it was a really good crowd)

    "Whole notion"
    to rebuke interpretation even while I perpetuate it

Preamble

Seated are the following: sports commentator Ariel Helwani, in buttoned-down blue tartan lumberjack shirt, voicing parenthetical deference; poet-critic Clint Burnham, slumped in chair, donning Irving Layton jewellery; poet John Ashbery, Mott St. Aloha shirt untucked over khaki shorts, beside a hen basket of Celestian Seasonings; victim of police brutality and author Rodney King, natty-casual, coiffed, photogenic.

Cameo appearances by: comedian Eugene Levy as novelist Elias Canetti, and vice-versa; Paris Communard Louise Michel, clearing throat to speak through a translation and not "pouting away in her bombazine gown" (Douglas Oliver); lesbian theorist

Monique Wittig as poet bill bissett as philosopher Simone de Beauvoir; theorist Kristin Ross, offstage; art critic Christine Poggi as performance-poet Elsa von Freytag-Loringhoven, in animation, seen above, breaking chandelier; essayist Lynne Segal, voiceover; the Faridabad Workers' News; theorist Jodi Dean, in blazing saddles and rearing horse; and poet Dorothy Trujillo Lusk, raising with both hands a snake's clump of greasy bicycle chains.

The darkened, inert figure in large cloak and hat, standing in corner throughout, is Fredric Jameson as Victor Hugo.

At one asynchronous moment, a Pavement lyric becomes audible.

Epilogue

No one knows, watching reports of the world summit, who any of these speakers are.

On the Continuity of English

*The ideology requires that English should be ancient
and pure with a continuous history.* — Jim Milroy

white dead
face set

      view mind
      impart virtue

one wind
feet night

      charms pomp
      various scenes

sang toward
laughed sea

      virtues arts
      pleasing muse

old bitter
mouth shadow

      every state
      appear powers

hair moon
things sun

      appears inspired
      rage formed

went eyes
rain dream

      claim superior
      native power

dawn blossom
men lips

      scene oft
      train attend

back dreamed
rose days

      fond join
      generous general

flower wherein
sake sunset

      different sincere
      boast nature

seeing sweet
love red

      pursue bestow
      force vain

grass stricken
blown apart

      sacred applause
      aid produce

morning singing
done yea

  retreat views
  relief zeal

thereof grew
nights again

  secure grandeur
  numbers numerous

made star
arisen heard

  transport extend
  repair displayed

honey faces
came thing

  joined taste
  supplied patriot

stars therein
maiden hands

  pride sage
  refined sway

nay drift
come strange

  remove crimes
  prospect engage

ways sunrise
till shut

  influence supply
  fortune social

as fro
kissed watch

     spleen leads
     ray dressed

gather kiss
life yesterday

     public attends
     employ grateful

surely bare
birds outer

     trace peculiar
     designed pleased

blowing hearted
bird water

     objects grove
     attention course

word last
thereon little

     display care
     passions science

looked grow
bride waiting

     rival genius
     supplies merit

north loving
broken leaves

demands seat
severe talents

RIBBON ENDS

struggle for "social
eval" ("recon")

      — gradual

                -ly as Lee

      — disguises — as

            Henry Lee Smith

     taste ("recog"

        (use of spacing, linebreak, m-dash & hyphen, open
        parenthesis, deletion, shortened word, name,
        homonym, lack
        of capitalization

        use of poetry, of print, use of cultural
        literacy, use of symbolic
        capital

structural

problem
use

of

"By *visible* [coconuts?] I mean those most
frequently constructed in anthologies and
criticism, and most successfully publicized and
commodified *as* [coconuts?] both outside and
within the geographic areas they claim to
[coconutize?]."

not independently mobile but decorative
functioning

in the back
round smokey hole

lending atmosphere
"ick" interest

capital
that nobody can deny

is
analogy

a jolly good
apologist will say

Coconuts?

Knocking
those
syllables

& who's
there

inside

I think

who's outside, laughter

I hear

— a joke?

or's (for doors)

all and's (on oars)

                 What have we of them,
        Or much or little? (1917)

"we use *or* and *or* and *nor* and *nor* in that way in poetry only and
        not in prose" (1865)

                    . . . hold your tongue, and let me love,
        Or chide my palsy, or my gout (1633)

                              hinges of
                              longing

                              nor

                              to join
                              hinges

A Real Alternative

and &s (& ands)

HERE'S WHAT WE KNOW AND DON'T KNOW

So, peacocks, these. Caj-like, they take off.
A Sunkist wake-up — white peacocks.
White and pissed.

I'm seeing white peacocks. As I start
snoozing, white peacocks
startle strolling. Caj-like peacocks, today.

Without doubt, fucking me up, these peacocks
lazing over to the pond,
cool shadow, outwaiting day.

(After "Ennui" by Maurice Maeterlinck)

Verminous reindeer
leap every way from Santa
vaselined, red nose — run, Rudolph

Dreamed, nothing
repaired, this morning
more sleep

No dreams, prams in trees
hospitals skulled, phrases
exploded girder

Hinges of
longing joined
to hinges

FUNNY

Thinking is for clowns

needing to worry

if the boss thinks

it

funny.

Good work. Set aside
We'll be in touch
when a structural
problem in your face-
work compromises
performance

WHO KEEPS CALLING ME? *GROAN*

>   Beijing &
Time —

>   Park early this time.

>   Fifteen the maximum pollution
Level —

>   Level four to three.

>   Teen Beat the number of exclamation
Marks —

>   Does terrorism have a   question
>   some   marks.

>   The compound <!————> in Herder's
Prose —

>   Prose was created before.

but manners
are trouble —

new manners &
no manners

   plus: hammers
in bags, duffle & tweed, hand

or shoulder, in suitcase or in rucksack,
& hamper & cake & pudding tins

bread box, bin, or barrel,
& the tiniest of hammers for a pencil case

        & also
nails, long & short, weighty & thin

for teeth, or feet, or arms
& with hammers for ears, & for eyes, & tongue

nail & tong
hammers all

for manners & meanwhile
a thing called a coffee table

& sitting, resisting
drinks & snacks, now & then eyes

coffee table
glancing off a book

#1.

(A & B speak without the raised inflection of the question-
mark and in identical manner — flat intonation — simulating a
rudimentary computer speech-synthesizer vernacular.)

A What you ok about. (*Pause.*)
B Nothing. (*Pause.*) You.
(*Pause.*)
A You. (*Pause.*)
B I'm nothing. (*Pause.*)
A I'm ok with nothing.
(*Pause.*)
B We ok with everything then. (*Pause.*)
A Not ok with that. (*Pause.*)
B You ok about what. (*Pause.*)
A Told you. (*Pause.*)
B Wait. (*Pause.*) Nothing.
(*Pause.*)
A You. (*Pause.*)
B Oh. (*Pause.*) I suppose. (*Pause.*)

~ Musical-numbers interlude. ~

#2.

(Animated voices.)

A (*Enunciates equally as poem and advertisement.*)

> NO PUNCTUATION NEED APPLY
> to 5.95 —
> period's decimal point:
> different!

B 5.95?
A See inside 5.95 — period's decimal point: different! See inside.
    See?
B 3.44?
A 3.44.
B 14.56!
A 14.56.

~ Musical–numbers interlude. ~

#3.

B Or 2.29.
A Or 2.29 . . . Wait, did you say 14.56?
B 14.56!
A I didn't realize. The exclamation nails it.
B The one-eighty.
A That's a good one.
B Money Mart next.
A Next to Starbucks . . .
B . . . Opposite Windsor Beauty . . .
A & B (*Rapturously*) . . . Su-p-p-lie-s! . . .
A Parking . . .
B . . . Lots. And lots . . . Home Depot, Walmart . . .
A Empty Rona building . . .
B That's a good one.

A It's Starbucks . . . (*Realizes*) Oh my Gordie Howe Bridge.
B Debit!
A The Starbucks Nihilists have it! . . . EATen . . .
A & B . . . the Star-Spangled Poutinistes!———
(*Pause.*)
B. Debit.

~ Musical-numbers interlude. ~

#4.

B 9:45.
A That's right.
B Gotta go.
A 11/16.
B That's right.
A Gotta go.
B That's right.
A 2016.
B Gotta go.
A That's right.
B Gotta go.
A Gotta go.

~ Musical-numbers extro. ~

Volutions

Past Tense

A town was built
on the verb to be.
That verb never arrived.
There already,
They celebrated.

Village yawns, economist
carefully plots it
along x-axis

a new day, with bees or
without them sun
eats planet

the way gasflame scours cast iron
under frying egg economist.
Villager taps window

shouts can't say
anything. Cocked-browed economist
lifts finger. His number mountain

needs atomic
calibration, not broom
villager waves.

Get real with your reality, mouths evidentiary villager.
Shouts threatening economist, I'd tear down this building only that
heavy elements on table, platonium such as, won't allow for my
   tantronium.

But his mind rallies. Do you think I like being a character
        imputing information.
I'm not going to be scripted by the every day.
There aren't fields enough to plant all numbers such as — need
        burial.

Shovel, villager mouths.
Strange, mimics sounding economist, what do you think dirt
        means, make corn blue.
Mouths villager, not strange.

Villager bends out of sight to re-tie loosened sack around foot.
Blue birds cut from sky, waxes economist,
collect in glass bowl

on this wooden table.
Jewels in dirt if you dig for, fracturing economist sounds
to his own ears as he calculates

volume in Russian dolls of mind, which doll encloses which
whether voice noise makes one volume or two.
This villager is coconut woven basket and has pleasant smell.

Pleased economist eats egg.
I don't have time for circles, only — gull cry — spheres.
Villager's got givens.

Gives gottens, I like that, ruminating economist shouts, do you
        think I'm allowed.
Miffing villager pouts a loud what, remember I'm obvious.
Loopholing economist writhes, languish if you want.

For verse to go, dig
do not call city.
Well, don't call my mother.

That's bad?
Villagers like signage.
Too.

Wish there were go signs.
No need: no
sign — means go.

Don't like signs for that reason, villager shouts in a way unlike
    villager.
Imagine spelling this backwards, is that what you want.
Can I interrupt, you remind me of the x-y axis.

Why don't you broaden shoulder.
Can't expect you to honour the chum.
It's for this reason I need talk, villager shouts — reader, you'd
    think, but economist shouts this.

Exaggerrating villager shouts wow, I'm expressed.
Does lake deserve friends.
I can't gas out.

Can you imagine plate glass like sun can.
Not through leaning.
Reader, they shout at each other.

I come full circle to nothing such as.
And: Just like your fried egg.
I'm looking at you through windowpane.

And: You make me feel not brand new.
Pants fall down.
And: Thankyou.

And: Morning disappears to birds flocking for song mnemonica.
> *peet-suh fitz-bee- wheek wheek*
> *gulp-a-pump woonk-a-chunk quack quack*
> *ka-ha; ka-ha kuh-uk!; kuh-uk!*

And: There's not a call I don't heed.
        poo-too-eee!; poo-too-eee!
        chwee; chwee; chwee pipit-pipit
        ka-brick ka-wheer prrrrt
And: Let me calibrate that for you.
        kyip; kyip; kyip
        maaagh?!
        wenk-wenk

        ch-wut
        too-fritchyoo-fritchyoo-fritchyoo
        kwuk

And: So that I can tie this knot for pants, squeeze here.
Economist opens window, *O Sweet Canada; Canada; Canada,*
        thinking about octopus, octopus escapes
three cubic centimeter volume

if Russian dolls four-deep inside little village (fishtanks).
I can't imagine paring life down to string.
The city relies on your calculations.

They don't care about my life, bursting economist reddens, not
        saddens.
Can't imagine they do, they care about mine, shouting villager
        brags.
I've been told that, at meetings, except I fall asleep at them and I
        don't know how they end.

There's birthing going on, we're not surprised.
I see tuna melt in your eye.
Economist shuts window, thinking about sun as pie would think
        about it, hot but necessary condition.

Clothe and send me on my way, I'm as ordinary as a basket and
        fond as a cat of it.
I can give you more than that, economist shouts.
Don't count on yourself.

I do, economist shouts, up to one villager such as.
I recognize myself by my number, shouting villager #1 asserts.
Don't believe we've met, remarks shouting economist as he butters
    slice of bread next.

You can't ask for more than that from people, shouts villager #1.
    Look at the cows, they're so that I'm awake most of the time.
Ambiguous phase, economist shouts.
I miss potato elites, growls ruminating villager.

Shall I calculate chips for you, offers homespinning shouting
    economist.
Boiling villager cries, make it a Tetley.
Time alert, form exists.

Nice to meet you, court won't admit.
I am myself telluric evidence for upset.
Trim pin.

Hungry Sling Shots

After *Les Nobles Triolets* (1647) by Saint-Amant

Triolet *tra la*
Truck a trio, let the triple trip, and tip
    Climate must be slightly lunatic
Triolet *tra la*
    Closed as open
Chance what places falls in place
    Triolet *tra la*
Truck a trio, let the triple trip, and tip

Those Greenwalds tickle
Flowering potato-green fruit
    De-ranged timbre, head noised up
Those Greenwalds tickle
    Hello anxiousness — going by truck
By gentle skinning, bare, sympathetic, ready
    Those Greenwalds tickle
Flowering potato-green fruit

Since there's bending
You feel it bent
   Apply for carnival *and* for protest
Since there's bending
   The Run for Sight
Recumbency makeover bent grass sort
   Since there's bending
You feel it bent

   River crowning
Unkneelable
   Mass trembling woke
River crowning
   Searching
Bridge His Majesty the Ego
   River crowning
Unkneelable

We see fish drown
Says Pierrette the beast
  In her street in a hundred ways
We see fish drown
  No hook, no line, no!
Shouting beast, beast
  We see fish drown
Says Pierrette the beast

  Forced weak
Those beg
  Without, withdrawn
Forced weak
  Who miss who
We're skinnying up
  Forced weak
Those beg

Fig nor raisin
Not an almond or hazelnut
    Says grocer our neighbour
Fig nor raisin
    Shelves are shelves
Says gazette
    Fig nor raisin
Not an almond or hazelnut

    Rice holeeee, none
With or without buildings
    Pea, bean, lentil, words
Rice holeeee, none
    Tears going all ways down to the top
I don't mock
    Holeeee, none
With or without buildings

    Hay and straw finish
We don't find it for double
    Wheat out
Hay and straw finish
    Wufflings and stares, ears prick forward
Yokes don't sit right
    Hay and straw finish
We don't find it for double

    Eat meat
Flies permit it in their sermons
    Do butcher laugh
Eat meat
    Heaps himself to throne
Sells dear, hirkling knows
    Eat meat
Flies permit it in their sermons

Abbey's ass
Re-live the biblical maybe
   Donkey burger
Abbey's ass
   And empty the small bottle
Revives poise
   Abbey's ass
Re-live the biblical maybe

One loaf — costs what?
Enlarge the loaf, escort the wheat
   Barricade this blockade
One loaf — costs what?
   Shield me baking 'round troups
When a tiny shield (TinyDuino legacies processor board)
                                        stamps silver
   One loaf — costs what?
Enlarge the loaf, escort the wheat

    Soon as grain comes alive in market
It goes
    Who's a good bagger, who bags for the rich
Soon as grain comes alive in market
    The visible and the invisible of it
Does what
    Soon as grain comes alive in market
It goes

    Appointed Representatives!
Regrates
    Pricing climbing into purse
Appointed Representatives!
    Bidders dealers
Pints in fine silver please
    Appointed Representatives!
Regrates

 Something they told me
Siege city
 Mind blanc
Something they told me
 Heart blocks
Tipping blood withon this block
 Something they told me
Siege city

 Divining
Had I sniffed the air, packed
 Parlanjhe! *Unbllie pa tun chapea*
Divining
 Wine, cheese, bread
Pawnways now the galligaskins
 Divining
Had I sniffed the air, packed

I love this councilor
At-just-the-right-angle trick
   "No longer sees what we're getting at"
I love this councilor
   Now hesitates near deeps (watercourse reclamation
                                    petition)
I do believe daylighting his face
   I love this councilor
At-just-the-right-angle trick

   Bring the drums
So brain me
   Downburbs from extown
Da dum
   Troll protest, dummies, ogres, effigies, dolls (did they
                                    ever exist?)
Made in rumours as Hebe, Esquire Under Siege,
                                    Evangelicals
   Bring the drums, hire their own Goliath
So brain me

To be in Canada, wherever that is
When I hear this rumpet
   A-hole in F-flat
To be in Canada, wherever that is
   My host moans
Lover who hurls, America
   To be in Canada, wherever that is
When I hear this rumpet

   Instead of curling iron
Sharpen tongue
   Airbending harp
Instead of curling iron
   Spit that bit
Retching, teach
   Instead of curling iron
Sharpen tongue

Make your case
As any two, spectate together
Crouching, standing
Make your case
·For better or what
Re specs, seeming likeness?
Make your case
As any two, spectate together

Hope's "therefore" sold
Trades trades for markets
Wait, there's more markets
Hope's "therefore" sold
This Side Only
Charlatans & suckers
Hope's "therefore" sold
Trades, for markets

Taken green and speechless
Neo-royale
    Worship to war shop flip
Taken green and speechless
    Risk and Hazard balk into a war
Whose to win loses — joke *flop*
    Taken green and speechless
Neo-royale

    Stunned
Mullet in Forbes "a fish is speaking"
    Foundry worker at clock movements
Stunned
    Me handle
By the throat, out of pocket
    Stunned
Mullet in Forbes "a fish is speaking"

Admirable effect — did you say admiral erect?
I hear admiral in the slishy slooshy waters of the tub
    Order *very* liberal, give thanks to the general!
Admiral select, but admirable?
    Give thanks to the general etc
We used the proper channels, slishy and slooshy
    Admirable — did you say admiral?
I hear admiral in the slishy slooshy waters of the tub

    Sovereign lunacies, blame the moon
'S over rain
    Mist want
Blame the moon
    Trance glaze
Cadaver tomb recumbency makeover
    Sovereign lunacies, blame the moon
'S over rain

Sedition by caprice and laughter
What don't yous readers say
    Imminent lawless action
Sedition by caprice and laughter
    Clear and present danger
Bad tendency
    Sedition by caprice and laughter
What don't yous readers say

    To arms *très sympa, les bourgeoisies*
A hundred tearful subjects
    Tip frost
To arms *très sympa, les bourgeoisies*
    Mars Bringer of Ēclairs to coffee shop wallpaper
Très sympa les bourgeoisies heh
    Forces the hand even / to arm the hands
A hundred tearful subjects

    Prepare to re-fold standard
Don't curse sober
    Partisan down!
Prepare to re-fold standard
    Party getting rough
Should toothpick flatten sparkle
    Prepare to re-fold standard
Don't curse sober

    When discussion turns
Proud person, discussion turns to shit
    Pityless — fire
When discussion turns
    Why don't we lose already
I lose my head
    When discussion turns
Proud person, discussion turns to shit

The end
Freak-outs
    Now it's difficult
The end
    The end of Chantilly lace, and tawdry from St. Audrey
Royal tears, no hanky, no mender
    The end
Freak-outs

    Nothing to translate here, keep to the line
A real lit wick
    Not much extra given
Keep to the line, nothing to translate here
    Powder into the breeches
Product tips to trough
    Nothing to translate here, keep the line
A real lit wick

All the same, reader, *Sorry*
In twenty seventeen — triolets
    What does that mean hacked my own firewall
All the same, reader, *Sorry*
    Light verse just got concert lighters
Troll living near drives honking til audible on livestream
    All the same, reader, *Sorry*
In twenty seventeen — triolets

    Surely offend no multinational
Poore inch of Nature
    Can I say like I feel
Surely offend no multinational
    To construct a triolet, climate must be lunatic
Prudent despite
    Surely offend no multinational
Poore inch of Nature

I don't toast *or* roast
Like O O O O bring me my tariffs
    Can you walk straight, external focal point
I don't toast *or* roast
    What's green, baked already
Not right stuffing, insides takeover
    I don't toast *or* roast, external focal point
Like ooooo bring me my tariffs

    That each imitate his every stet
Original future, our Not
    "Abundance for the few"
That each imitate his every stet
    Whiteness mans into world economic labyrinth
Chicken Charlie boils — the shoelace
    That each imitate his every stet
Original future, our Not

The Teniers, maggots
Paints peasants
   Carnival: 'The King Drinks'
The Teniers, maggots
   Milder weather, vulnerable state
Archduke — buys Winter
   The Teniers
Keeper of the art — paints peasants

   Snow con serves the lily
Definite article
   What is the lily
Snow con serves the lily
   Giglio's SnoCone
Their common whiteness
   Snow con serves the lily
Definite article

Courage, turning point
Concrete, asphalt and dirt lots, dust and diesel, we call it
                                        a parade
    Falling, pushed, or pulled into trucking
Courage, turning point
    Breaker One Nine this here's Rubber Duck?
Congratulations, you meet our minimal requirements!
    Courage, turning point
Concrete, asphalt and dirt lots, dust and diesel, we call it
                                        a parade

    Cow power coming LIVE LOAD
And donkey charge, sacks to go
    Flour, cabbage, onion, turnip
Cow power coming LIVE LOAD
    Express the functions in services-to-be-provided
Use-functions and less-important esteem-functions
    LVLD: W32475, W32476, W32477
And donkey charge, sacks to go

Enter from every street
Horned beasts
   Pigs and sheep, from every field
Enter from every street
   Grim — no more — macabre
Rampart dancing
   Enters from every street
Horned beasts

   Each their own Capitaine
Crazy panache, they start, they laugh
   Cruel eyes steaming biscuits
Each their own Capitaine
   Coming on
Slurp, drool, chomp, grin, drool
   Each their own Capitaine
They start, they laugh — crazy panache

Norman the operator's with us
Doesn't "deduct" services, he stirs them in!
    Allegoresis
Norman the operator's with us
    To drink a fine cider
To the draining of accounts
    Norman the operator's with it
Doesn't "deduct" services, he stirs them in!

    Rare song
Richer libel
    Between eight and nine on the bridge
Rare song
    Brown egg sack paper verse
Why the punk rocker crossed the road
    Rare song
Richer libel

To secure liberty they will say
Chain the city
    By the extremes (are not unknowns)
To secure liberty they will say
    Yes Your Majesty Sir
Please harness my mouth
    To secure liberty they will say
Chain the city

    In this tasteful way
Doin' the Mazaniello, last nine days
    While asleep in their condoms, minions of government
In this tasteful way
    No ideas but in wealthy taxpayers
There are few wealthy taxpayers
    In this tasteful way
Doin' the Mazaniello, last nine days

To catch a bilker
Marvel
    What dilligence
To catch a bilker
    To checkmate by pawn
To win a lottery
    Catch a bilker
Marvel

    U.S. envoy arrives
Sent from my coal powered iPad
    You feel very important
U.S. envoy arrives
    You feel very naked as usual
Atwood and Munro on the reading list
    U.S. envoy arrives
Sent from my coal powered iPad

More unborn
A certain and verifiable record
Whether mother X or Y
More unborn
Not working or spending
Not In Service
More unborn
A certain and verifiable record

Tycoon plants straightface
What a plant, not green
Loophole loop holds loop / hole over sight
Tycoon plants straightface
Fake noose, loop holds
Trending word lookups, clemency, treason
Tycoon plants straightface
What a plant, not green

Words cross at going purposes
Things pursed
    Inside one as in another
Words cross at going purposes
    Thing going into purse
Words crossed for going purse
    Words cross at going purposes
Things pursed

    To the poets
Wreathe's petal, nettle
    Cruel act, cries of help
To the poets
    A fronted say
Who loves chafes
    Through the poets
Wreathe's nettle

Enemy suspended, officially
Escapade ovations
    Theirs confused with ours
Enemy suspended, officially
    Meanwhile, ground reddens
By one as by the other
    Enemy suspended, officially
Escapade ovations

    Vulnerable *wound*
It's the acting
    Please like me
Vulnerable *wound*
    Because or *But*
Reason makes what takes
    Vulnerable *wound*
It's the acting

Out of place
So Louis put in his
    Who wants place
Out of place
    This word
And *must* got personal
    Out of place
So Louis put in his

    Enough privilege
Thermostat, dimmers and fan controls
    Inside what
Enough privilege
    Slogan ear
"People" hot
    Enough privilege
Thermostat, dimmers and fan controls

Fear of left behind
Go right leaves behind
    Don't give up, down only
Fear of left behind
    Don't kneel *by kneeling*
Argue the quibble there already
    Fear of left behind
Go right leaves behind

    Speak up to down, speak in
No Reply, should I hope for anything else
    Show to come, talk to go
Speak out, speak down to up, speak in
    Words, appear
In their element — what's mine
    Speak up to down, speak in
No Reply, should I hope for anything else

Understood but
What, the finger's the eye
   Voice-creep
Understood but
   That way, you see?
You're responsive, you respond
   Understood but
What, the finger's the eye

   Forces grimace
There makeup?
   Concealer then foundation, word then situation
Forces grimace
   Check yourself
No see-through
   Forces grimace
There makeup?

Keep it elevated, members of parliament, remember,
                                        you're members
Those who follow re-member you whole
  Other love, no other other love
Elevated members of parliament, remember, you're
                                        members
  Hungry slingshots your embers
Remember us for this dissatisfaction
  Keep it elevated, members of parliament, remember,
                                        you're members
Those who follow mistaken you whole

        (perversion version)

  Olive branch our laurel
Break it off, poets
  New flavour-science
Olive branch our laurel
  Awards chain, break it up
From the air, a live
  Olive branch our laurel
Break it off, poets

Closed as open
Pass for illustration
    When ear is close
Das open!!
    Say-through manoeuver
As if the whole of nature were as senseless as they are
    Closed as open
Pass for illustration

    People greet
What-else to say . . . rituals re-form
    Speak, nevertheless, to the end
People greet
    Easing agrammatical, factual
Tears well, from another, laughter
    People greet
What-else to say . . . rituals re-form

torn

an invisible entertainment
somehow
falls upon all things

— R. Blaser

"In the process and function of democracy there is something missing, the figure of the king, whose death, I believe, fundamentally, the people did not want … created an emotional void."
— Emmanuel Macron, *Le 1*

"The degree of economic exploitation guaranteed by French Absolutism can be judged by the recent calculation that throughout the 17th century, the nobility — 2 per cent of the population — appropriated 20-30 per cent of the total national income."
— Perry Anderson, *Lineages of the Absolutist State*

Even by a conservative revision of the Thomas Piketty estimate in *Capital in the Twenty-First Century*, concentration in the top 1 per cent of total U.S. wealth and income in 2012 is estimated at just under 34%.

Air

In various places at accidental times
the good lines

I've read, looking to a scrap, listening
at this scratch again

at the scrap, then to the scratch,
then scrap,

scratch —
if only someone collected the good lines

"reading the past exclusively through
the present," what lines

presented with such "presentism" here
would a present gift

in this occluded space (polished up of course
if I work it, scratchy pen

"not actual size," so too the used paper)
if I ask, act critical, scratching out, scrapping

what remains, what
are they, "remains"

below, out of my depths, looking
to, listening at, also listening

out, while looking up, and — look,
from reversals within the

phrase "looking and listening," combined
with "to," "at," "out," "up,"

maybe you want to anticipate the next combo
(what? *is* it? and is *it* moozical?): listen

(but also *don't* listen: ignore, cringe
not listening, *not* "listening down," *not* looking, definitely not
    "looking in")

to a repetition formalized in verse **so**
to pull from these currents a Flopsy, a Mopsy, a Dopesy

if only this would end at the preverbal rabbits
and in various places at accidental times.

Notes on the Poems

"The Mommy Collection"
The series began while translating Théodore de Banville's *Roses de Noël* (1879) and a few poems from his first book, *Les Cariatides* (1842). I used the second edition of Banville's collected works published by Alphonse Lemerre in 1889 and also volume VI of the 1999 critical edition Peter J. Edwards oversaw for Honoré Champion. The Errol Morris epigraph transcribes bytes from Preet Bharara's interview podcasted November 7, 2019 on *Stay Tuned with Preet*. The phrases "This category of France's 'lie'" and "the mother contends with the sky" I borrow from William Carlos Williams's *Spring and All*. ROS is a robot operating system and a metaplasm of rose. "Arques! Arques! Des docks doux, barques" is a line from *N'Heures Souris Rames: The Coucy Castle Manuscript* by Ormonde de Kay (Clarkson N. Potter, Inc., Publishers, 1980). "Make liberals cry again": t-shirt slogan, circa 2020 U.S.A.

"The Bromeliad"
The epigraph modifies a sample sentence about the plant, which I found at ReversoContext. "And out of the cups . . . . thunder-showers": couplet from Percy Bysshe Shelley's "The Sensitive Plant."

"On the Continuity of English"
Largely consists of content words (nouns, verbs, adjectives) correlating most and least (most or "top" 100 words in the left column, least or "bottom" 100 in the right) with a pre-/post-1150 A.D. word-origins ratio tabulated annually from 1755 to 1900 out of the 10,000 most common words in the British poetry canon. This tabulation was done by Ted Underwood, helped by Jordan Sellers ("Etymology and nineteenth-century poetic diction," tedunderwood.com). Underwood determines that words with pre-1150 origins are on average 2.5 times more prevalent in poetry than in nonfiction prose. The epigraph is from Jim Milroy's Prologue to *Alternative Histories of English*, edited by Richard Watts and Peter Trudgill, Routledge, 2002.

"Ribbon Ends"
"Mainstream Exoticology," original quotation is by Frank Davey, "Toward the Ends of Regionalism" (*Textual Studies in Canada* 9, Spring 1997). "Canned": Gerard Manley Hopkins in "On the Origins of Beauty" writes about the poetic *or*; sample usages are Ezra Pound and John Donne.

"Hungry Sling Shots"
Began as a translation of *Les Nobles Triolets* (1647) by Saint-Amant (Marc-Antoine Girard, Sieur de Saint-Amant, 1594-1661), whose poems I discovered researching the triolet and other forms popular during the Fronde civil war for an essay on Ted Greenwald's poetry. Saint-Amant composed a sequence of 64 triolets during the royal military blockade of Paris which he experienced as a house-bound invalid. I used Jean Lagny's 1969 critical edition, *Oeuvres*, vol. III, Librairie Marcel Didier. "bare, sympathetic, ready": Robert Duncan's words from *The H.D. Book* (edited by Victor Coleman and Michael Boughn, U of California P, 2011). "Parlanjhe" is the French Poitevin dialect spoken in Poitou. "dummies, ogres, effigies, dolls (did they ever exist?)": modified from H.D.'s *Tribute to Freud*. "Forbes" is poet John Forbes, "The Stunned Mullet" in the book by that name (Hale & Iremonger, 1988). "Sedition by caprice and laughter" is what Diderot said of *frondeur* literati. "Poore inch of Nature": Shakespeare quoted by Freud in *Civilization and Its Discontents*. "The Teniers" is the painting "Carnival: 'The King Drinks'" (oil on copper, 1690) by David Teniers the Younger, who also painted an allegorical portrait called "Winter" (oil on copper, 1644). "Concrete, asphalt and dirt lots . . . . trucking" and the line "Congratulations . . ." are from Steve Viscelli, *The Big Rig* (U of California P, 2016). "Remember us for this dissatisfaction" is in a war poem of Robin Blaser's *The Holy Forest*. "From the air / a live": once-famous poets' bespoke from Ezra Pound (Canto 81). "As if the whole of nature were as senseless as they are": Spinoza, *Theological-Political Treatise*, translated by Michael Silverthorne and Jonathan Isreal. Film still: Jean Cocteau's *Testament of Orpheus* (1959).

"Air"
Peter Barry defines presentism as, "reading the past exclusively through the present" (*Beginning Theory*, Manchester UP, 2009).

Acknowledgements

I am grateful to South Bay Birders Unlimited, Palo Alto CA, for their online list of bird-sound mnemonics. Thanks to the editors of *BOO*, *Canada and Beyond: A Journal of Canadian and Literary Studies*, *Generation*, *Partial Zine*, *Some*, *ti-TCR: a web folio*, and *Yellow Field*, where some of these poems or where versions of these poems appeared. I'd like to thank funk-étude quartet leader Catriona Strang, and members Michael Barnholden and Colin Smith. I'd like to thank the university outside the university, and chancellors Ted Byrne and Donato Mancini. I'd like to thank curator Steven Tong for including the triolet "Understood but . . ." in the exhibition "How to Read a Window" at PLAZA Projects, Richmond BC, August 2017. Thank you to Rolf Maurer, publisher with social critique, and his European modernist accomplice, Vladimir Cristache, and Oliver McPartlin, whose Spring swatch sample rivals Charles Demuth's. Especialemente, deep gratitude to Rob Manery for generous commentary and for meticulous interior designwork on the book. I owe everything to Nicole Markotić and her marvelously gnarly editorial and poetry imagination, and her tenacity, charm and pop, through countless drafts and conversations.